Anonymous

Statutes of Columbia College and its Associated Schools

Vol. 1

Anonymous

Statutes of Columbia College and its Associated Schools
Vol. 1

ISBN/EAN: 9783337372798

Printed in Europe, USA, Canada, Australia, Japan

Cover: Foto ©ninafisch / pixelio.de

More available books at **www.hansebooks.com**

STATUTES

OF

COLUMBIA COLLEGE

AND

ITS ASSOCIATED SCHOOLS:

TO WHICH ARE ADDED,

THE PERMANENT RESOLUTIONS

AND

ORDERS OF THE BOARD OF TRUSTEES.

NEW YORK:
D. VAN NOSTRAND, PUBLISHER,
23 MURRAY AND 27 MURRAY STREET.

1874.

CONTENTS.

—:o:—

	PAGE
Trustees of Columbia College	7
Standing Committee	8
Committee on the Course of Instruction	8
Committee on the School of Mines	8
Committee on the School of Law	9
Committee on the Library	9
Committee on Honors	9
Faculty of Arts	10
Other Officers of the College	11
Faculty of the School of Mines	12
Other Officers of the School of Mines	12
Faculty of the School of Law	13
Lecturers in the School of Law	13
Faculty of the School of Medicine	14
Other Officers of the School of Medicine	15
Trustees of the Medical Department	16
Historical Sketch of Columbia College	17

STATUTES OF THE COLLEGE.

CHAPTER I.
Of the President 25

CHAPTER II.
Of the Board of the College 26

CHAPTER III.
Of the Course of Study 28

CONTENTS.

	PAGE
CHAPTER IV.	
Of Admission	30
CHAPTER V.	
Of Attendance	32
CHAPTER VI.	
Of Discipline	32
CHAPTER VII.	
Of the Proficiency of the Students	33
CHAPTER VIII.	
Of Examinations for Honors	36
CHAPTER IX.	
Of Commencements	37
CHAPTER X.	
Of Vacations	38
CHAPTER XI.	
Of the Library	39
CHAPTER XII.	
Of Free Scholarships	40
CHAPTER XIII.	
Of Foundations	41

STATUTE ORGANIZING THE SCHOOL OF MINES.

CHAPTER I.	
Of the President	43
CHAPTER II.	
Of the Faculty of the School of Mines	43
CHAPTER III.	
Of Discipline	44
CHAPTER IV.	
Of Fees for Tuition	45

CONTENTS.

STATUTE ORGANIZING THE SCHOOL OF LAW.

PAGE

CHAPTER I.
Of the President.. 47

CHAPTER II.
Of the Warden... 47

CHAPTER III.
Of the Faculty of Law.. 48

CHAPTER IV.
Of Discipline.. 49

RESOLUTIONS PROVIDING FOR A SCHOOL OF MEDICINE.

RESOLUTION I.
College of Physicians and Surgeons adopted as the School of Medicine... 51

RESOLUTION II.
Manner of Conferring Degrees..................................... 51

RESOLUTION III.
Reservation of Power to Dissolve the Relation.................... 51

MISCELLANEOUS RESOLUTIONS.

Resolutions concerning the College............................... 52
Resolutions concerning the School of Mines....................... 54
Resolutions concerning the School of Law......................... 56
Resolutions creating the Committee on the Library................ 58
Resolutions relating to Diplomas................................. 60
Resolution concerning Emeritus Professors........................ 61

RULES AND ORDERS CONCERNING PRIZES.

Prizes in the College.. 63
Prizes in the School of Law...................................... 67
Prizes in the School of Medicine................................. 71

RULES OF ORDER.

	PAGE
General Regulations	73
Chapel Regulations	74
Regulations of the Library	77

COLUMBIA COLLEGE.

Board of Trustees.

NAMES.	RESIDENCES.
HAMILTON FISH, LL. D., CHAIRMAN OF THE BOARD.	251 East 17th Street.
SAMUEL B. RUGGLES, LL. D.	24 Union Square.
WM. BETTS, LL. D., CLERK.	122 East 30th Street.
BENJAMIN I. HAIGHT, S. T. D., LL. D.	56 West 26th "
ROBERT RAY	363 West 28th "
GOUVERNEUR M. OGDEN, TREASURER.	187 Fulton, h. 84 West 11th "
HENRY J. ANDERSON, M. D., LL. D.	60 Park Avenue.
EDWARD L. BEADLE, M. D.	Poughkeepsie.
GEORGE T. STRONG	113 East 21st Street.
MANCIUS S. HUTTON, S. T. D.	47 East Ninth "
HORATIO POTTER, S. T. D., LL. D., D. C. L.	38 East 22d "
LEWIS M. RUTHERFURD	175 Second Avenue.
THOMAS DE WITT, S. T. D.	55 East Ninth Street.
JOHN C. JAY, M. D	Rye, or 24 West 48th "
WILLIAM C. SCHERMERHORN	49 West 23d "
MORGAN DIX, S. T. D.	27 West 25th "
FREDERICK A. P. BARNARD, S. T. D., LL. D., L. H. D.,	College Green.
SAMUEL BLATCHFORD, LL. D.	12 West 22d Street.
STEPHEN P. NASH	11 West 19th "
CHARLES R. SWORDS	156 Broadway.
ANTHONY HALSEY	291 Broadway.
JOSEPH W. HARPER	231 Pearl Street.
CORNELIUS R. AGNEW, M. D	244 Madison Ave.
EVERT A. DUYCKINCK	20 Clinton Place.

Committees of the Trustees.

STANDING COMMITTEE.

NAMES.	RESIDENCES.
GOUVERNEUR M. OGDEN, Chairman	84 West 11th Street.
WILLIAM BETTS, LL. D	122 East 30th "
CHARLES R. SWORDS	156 Broadway.
WILLIAM C. SCHERMERHORN	49 West 23d Street.
ANTHONY HALSEY	291 Broadway.
JOSEPH W. HARPER	231 Pearl Street.

COMMITTEE ON THE COURSE OF INSTRUCTION.

NAMES.	RESIDENCES.
HORATIO POTTER, S. T. D., LL. D., D. C. L	38 East 22d Street.
MORGAN DIX, S. T. D	27 West 25th "
GEORGE T. STRONG	113 East 21st "
LEWIS M. RUTHERFURD	175 Second Avenue.
FREDERICK A. P. BARNARD, S. T. D., LL. D., L. H. D.,	College Green.

COMMITTEE ON THE SCHOOL OF MINES.

NAMES.	RESIDENCES.
WILLIAM BETTS, LL. D., Chairman	122 East 30th Street.
GEORGE T. STRONG	113 East 21st "
LEWIS M. RUTHERFURD	175 Second Avenue.
FREDERICK A. P. BARNARD, S. T. D., LL. D., L. H. D.,	College Green.
HAMILTON FISH, LL. D	251 East 17th Street.

COMMITTEES OF THE TRUSTEES.

COMMITTEE ON THE SCHOOL OF LAW.

NAMES.	RESIDENCES.
SAMUEL B. RUGGLES, LL. D., CHAIRMAN	24 Union Square.
HAMILTON FISH, LL. D.	251 East 17th Street.
GOUVERNEUR M. OGDEN, ESQ.	84 West 11th "
GEORGE T. STRONG, ESQ.	113 East 21st "
WILLIAM BETTS, LL. D	122 East 30th "
SAMUEL BLATCHFORD, LL. D	12 West 22d "
STEPHEN P. NASH	11 West 19th "
THEODORE W. DWIGHT, LL. D	8 Great Jones "

COMMITTEE ON THE LIBRARY.

NAMES.	RESIDENCES.
HENRY J. ANDERSON, M. D., LL. D., CHAIRMAN	60 Park Avenue.
GEORGE T. STRONG	113 East 21st Street.
WILLIAM C. SCHERMERHORN	49 West 23d "
FREDERICK A. P. BARNARD, S. T. D., LL. D. L. H. D.	College Green.
BENJAMIN I. HAIGHT, S. T. D., LL. D	56 West 26th Street.
BEVERLEY R. BETTS, CLERK	122 East 30th "

COMMITTEE ON HONORS.

NAMES.	RESIDENCES.
WILLIAM BETTS, LL. D., CHAIRMAN	122 East 30th Street.
HORATIO POTTER, S. T. D., LL. D., D. C. L	38 East 22d "
HENRY J. ANDERSON, M. D., LL. D	60 Park Avenue.
GEORGE T. STRONG	113 East 21st Street.
FREDERICK A. P. BARNARD, S. T. D., LL. D., L. H. D.	College Green.

Faculty of Arts.

NAMES.   RESIDENCES.

FREDERICK A. P. BARNARD, S. T. D., LL.D., L. H. D. Columbia College.
President.

HENRY JAMES ANDERSON, LL. D............60 Park Avenue.
Emeritus Professor of Mathematics and Astronomy.

HENRY DRISLER, LL. D.......................48 West 46th Street.
Jay Professor of the Greek Language and Literature.

HENRY I. SCHMIDT, S. T. D...................126 West 43d "
Gebhard Professor of the German Language and Literature.

CHARLES A. JOY, Ph. D.......................Columbia College.
Professor of Chemistry.

CHARLES DAVIES, LL. D......................Fishkill Landing.
Emeritus Professor of the Higher Mathematics.

WILLIAM G. PECK, LL. D.....................126 East 35th Street.
Professor of Mathematics and Astronomy.

CHARLES MURRAY NAIRNE, L. H. D..........163 West 34th "
Professor of Moral and Intellectual Philosophy and English Literature.

JOHN H. VAN AMRINGE, A. M.................140 East 44th Street.
Professor of Mathematics and Secretary of the Faculty.

OGDEN N. ROOD, A. M........................341 East 15th "
Professor of Mechanics and Physics.

CHARLES SHORT, LL. D......................24 West 60th "
Professor of the Latin Language and Literature.

Other Officers.

NAMES.	RESIDENCES.
CORNELIUS R. DUFFIE, S. T. D. .... Chaplain.	233 Lexington Av.
BEVERLEY R. BETTS, A. M. .... Librarian.	122 East 30th St.
AUGUSTUS C. MERRIAM, A. M. .... Tutor in Latin and Greek.	491 Fifth Av.
JOHN D. QUACKENBOS, A. B. .... Tutor in Rhetoric and History.	331 West 28th St.
EDWARD JOHN HALLOCK, A. M. .... Assistant in General Chemistry.	115 East 56th St.
LEONARD WALDO, B. S. .... Assistant in the Astronomical Observatory.	Columbia College.
JOHN H. VAN AMRINGE, A. M. .... Secretary of the Faculty.	140 East 44th St.
CHARLES A. CUSHMAN .... Secretary to the President.	419 West 19th St.
WILLIAM H. WALTER, Mus. D. .... Organist.	Fordham, N. Y.
STEPHEN R. WEEKS .... Janitor and Assistant Librarian.	Columbia College.

Faculty of the School of Mines.

NAMES.	RESIDENCES.
FREDERICK A. P. BARNARD, S. T. D., LL.D., L. H. D.	Columbia College.
President.	
THOMAS EGLESTON, Jr., A. M., E. M.	10 Fifth Av.
Professor of Mineralogy and Metallurgy.	
FRANCIS L. VINTON, E. M	St. Dennis Hotel.
Professor of Mining Engineering.	
CHARLES F. CHANDLER, Ph. D, M. D., LL.D.	51 East 54th St.
Dean of the Faculty, and Professor of Analytical and Applied Chemistry	
CHARLES A. JOY, Ph. D	Columbia College.
Professor of General Chemistry.	
WILLIAM G. PECK, LL.D	126 East 35th St.
Professor of Mechanics.	
JOHN H. VAN AMRINGE, A. M.	140 East 44th St.
Professor of Mathematics.	
OGDEN N. ROOD, A. M	341 East 15th St.
Professor of Physics.	
JOHN S. NEWBERRY, M. D., LL. D	Columbia College.
Professor of Geology and Paleontology.	

Other Officers.

FREDERICK STENGEL, A. M	51 East 20th St.
Instructor in German.	
JULES E. LOISEAU	2 East 33d St.
Instructor in French.	
HENRY CARRINGTON BOLTON, A. M., Ph. D	49 West 51st St.
Assistant in Analytical Chemistry.	
ELWYN WALLER, A. M., E. M.	33 West 15th St.
Assistant in Analytical Chemistry.	
ALEXIS A. JULIEN, A. M	110 East 80th St.
Assistant in Analytical Chemistry.	
FREDERICK A. CAIRNS, A. M	40 Grove St.
Assistant in Analytical Chemistry.	

OTHER OFFICERS.

WILLIAM PISTOR, E. M............................Columbia College.
    Assistant in Drawing.
HENRY NEWTON, A. B., E. M....................26 West 21st St.
    Assistant in Geology.
PIERRE DE PEYSTER RICKETTS, E. M..........32 East 74th St.
    Assistant in Assaying.
CHARLES ADAMS COLTON, E. M................748 Fifth St.
    Assistant in Mineralogy.
EDWARD JOHN HALLOCK, A. M................115 East 56th St.
    Assistant in General Chemistry.
JOHN KROM REES, A. B..........................303 East 17th St.
    Assistant in Mathematics.
WILLIAM HALSEY INGERSOLL, A. M., LL. B....105 East 21st St.
    Assistant in Civil Engineering.
JOHN F. MEYER ....41 Horatio St.
    Registrar and Librarian.
CHARLES RICHTER, Janitor......................Columbia College.

Faculty of the School of Law.

FREDERICK A. P. BARNARD, S. T. D., LL.D., L. H. D. Columbia College.
    President.
THEODORE W. DWIGHT, LL. D ....8 Great Jones Street.
    Warden of the Law School, and Professor of Municipal Law.
———————, ——————...................
    Professor of Constitutional History and Public Law.
CHARLES MURRAY NAIRNE, L. H. D..........163 West 34th Street.
    Professor of the Ethics of Jurisprudence.
JOHN ORDRONAUX, M. D., LL. D................Roslyn, L. I.
    Professor of Medical Jurisprudence.

Lecturers.

CHARLES P. DALY, LL. D ....84 Clinton Place.
GEORGE H. YEAMAN.............................306 Broadway.
CHARLES F. MACLEAN...........................12 East 12th Street.

JANITOR.

FELIX CURTIS ....8 Great Jones Street.

Faculty of the School of Medicine.

EDWARD DELAFIELD, M. D.,
President.

WILLARD PARKER, M. D.,
Professor of Clinical Surgery.

ALONZO CLARK, M. D.,
Professor of Pathology and Practical Medicine.

JOHN C. DALTON, M. D.
Professor of Physiology and Hygiene.

SAMUEL ST. JOHN, M. D.,
Professor of Chemistry and Medical Jurisprudence.

THOMAS M. MARKOE, M. D.,
Professor of Surgery.

T. GAILLARD THOMAS, M. D.,
Professor of Obstetrics and the Diseases of Women and Children.

JOHN T. METCALFE, M. D.,
Professor of Clinical Medicine.

HENRY B. SANDS, M. D.,
Professor of Anatomy.

JAMES W. McLANE, M. D.,
Adjunct Professor of Obstetrics and the Diseases of Women and Children.

THOMAS T. SABINE, M. D.,
Adjunct Professor of Anatomy.

CHARLES F. CHANDLER, Ph. D.
Adjunct Professor of Chemistry and Medical Jurisprudence.

EDWARD CURTIS, M. D.,
Professor of Materia Medica and Therapeutics.

WILLIAM DETMOLD, M. D.,
Emeritus Professor of Clinical and Military Surgery.

WILLIAM H. DRAPER, M. D.,
Clinical Professor of Diseases of the Skin.

CORNELIUS R. AGNEW, M. D.,
Clinical Professor of Diseases of the Eye and Ear.

ABRAHAM JACOBI, M. D.,
Clinical Professor of Diseases of Children.

FESSENDEN N. OTIS, M. D.,
Clinical Professor of Venereal Diseases.

JOHN G. CURTIS, M. D.,
Demonstrator of Anatomy.

CHARLES McBURNEY, M. D.,
Assistant Demonstrator of Anatomy.

Other Officers.

JAMES L. LITTLE, M. D.,
Lecturer on Operative Surgery and Surgical Dressings.

GEORGE G. WHEELOCK, M. D.,
Lecturer on Physical Diagnosis.

A. BRAYTON BALL, M. D.,
Lecturer on Diseases of the Kidneys.

FRANCIS DELAFIELD, M. D.,
Lecturer on Pathological Anatomy.

ROBERT F. WEIR, M. D.,
Lecturer on Diseases of the Male Pelvic Organs.

JOHN G. CURTIS, M. D.,
Lecturer on Injuries and Diseases of the Blood-vessels.

CLINICAL ASSISTANTS.

JAMES L. LITTLE, M. D.	A. BRAYTON BALL, M. D.
JOHN T. KENNEDY, M. D.	ALBERT H. BUCK, M. D.
GERARDUS H. WYNKOOP, M. D.	LUCIUS D. BULKLEY, M. D.
HENRY F. WALKER, M. D.	THOS. E. SATTERTHWAITE, M. D
CHARLES S. WARD, M. D.	THOMAS A. McBRIDE, M. D.
ROBERT W. TAYLOR, M. D.	FRANK P. KINNICUTT, M. D.
FRANCIS DELAFIELD, M. D.	ISAAC ADLER, M. D.
W. DE FOREST DAY, M. D.	SAMUEL B. St. JOHN, M. D.
WOOLSEY JOHNSON, M. D.	ROBERT F. WEIR, M. D.
OREN D. POMEROY, M. D.	

GEORGE B. FOWLER, M. D.
Curator of the College Museum.

EDWARD T. BOAG,
Clerk of the College.

ANDREW LOUGHLIN,
Janitor.

Trustees of the Medical Department.

EDWARD DELAFIELD, M. D. ....President.
EDWARD L. BEADLE, M. D. ....Vice-President.
ELLSWORTH ELIOT, M. D ....Registrar.
CAMBRIDGE LIVINGSTON ....Treasurer.

Trustees.

EDWARD G. LUDLOW, M. D.	CAMBRIDGE LIVINGSTON.
EDWARD DELAFIELD, M. D.	JARED LINSLY, M. D.
JOHN P. CROSBY.	JOHN J. CRANE, M. D.
GURDON BUCK, M. D.	ELLSWORTH ELIOT, M. D.
DANIEL D. LORD.	JAMES L. BANKS, M. D.
JAMES W. BEEKMAN.	ROBERT G. REMSEN.
BENJAMIN R. WINTHROP.	GEORGE D. H. GILLESPIE.
EDWARD L. BEADLE, M. D.	EDWARD H. LUDLOW.
Hon. F. A. CONKLING.	EDWARD DELAFIELD, Jr.
Rev. SULLIVAN H. WESTON, D.D.	WILLARD PARKER, M. D.
WILLIAM BETTS.	JOHN G. ADAMS, M. D.

CHARLES CLARKSON GOODHUE.

HISTORICAL SKETCH

OF

COLUMBIA COLLEGE.

The establishment of a college in the city of New York, was many years in agitation before the design was carried into effect. At length, under an act of Assembly, passed in December, 1746, and other similar acts which followed, moneys were raised by public lottery " for the encouragement of learning, and towards the founding a college " within the colony. These moneys were, in November, 1751, vested in trustees; of whom, ten in number, seven were members of the Church of England, and some of these seven were also vestrymen of Trinity Church.

These circumstances, together with the liberal grant of land to the college by Trinity Church, excited apprehensions of a design to introduce a church-establishment within the province, and caused violent opposition to the plan, as soon as it became known, of obtaining a royal charter for the college.

This opposition, however, being at last in a great measure surmounted, the trustees in November, 1753, invited Dr. Samuel Johnson, of Connecticut, to be President of the intended college. Dr. Johnson consequently removed to New York in the month of April following, and in July, 1754, commenced the instruction of a class of students in a room of the school-house belonging to Trinity Church; but he would not absolutely accept of the Presidency until after the passing of the charter. This took place on the 31st of October in the same year, 1754; from which period the existence of the college is properly to be dated. The governors of the college, named in the charter, are the archbishop of Canterbury, and the first Lord commissioner for trade and plantations, both empowered to act by proxies; the lieutenant-governor of the province, and several other public officers; together with the rector of Trinity Church, the senior minister of the Reformed Protestant Dutch Church, the ministers of the German Lutheran Church, of the French Church, of the Presbyterian Congregation, and the president of the college, all *ex officio*, and twenty-four of the principal gentlemen of the city. The college was to be known by the name of *King's College*. Previously to the passing of the charter, a parcel of ground to the westward of Broadway, bounded by Barclay, Church, and Murray streets, and by the Hudson river, had been destined by the vestry of Trinity Church as a site for the college edifice; and, accordingly, after the charter was granted, a grant of the land was made, on the 13th of May, 1755. On a portion of this plot, at the foot of Upper Robinson street, as it was at first called, but afterwards Park place, the college was subsequently built, and there stood for one hundred and three years, until its removal to another site, in 1857, occasioned by the demands of the business of the city. The part of the land thus granted by Trinity Church, not occupied for college purposes, was leased, and became a very valuable endowment to the college.

The sources whence the funds of the institution were derived besides the proceeds of the lotteries above mentioned, were the voluntary contributions of private individuals in this country, and sums obtained by agents who were subsequently sent to England and France. In May, 1760, the college buildings began to be occupied. In March, 1763, Dr. Johnson resigned his office of president, and the Rev. Dr. Myles Cooper, of Oxford, who had previously been appointed Professor of Moral Philosophy, and assistant to the president, was elected in his place. In 1767, a grant of land was obtained, under the government of Sir Henry Moore, of twenty-four thousand acres, situated in the northern parts of the province of New York; but by the terms of the treaty which the State of New York concluded with Vermont upon its erection into a separate state, this among other grants of land lying within its limits, was annulled, and the college consequently lost a tract of great value, inasmuch as it constituted the county town of the county in which it was situated.

In August, of the year 1767, a medical school was established in the college.

The following account of the institution, supposed to be written by Dr. Cooper, shows its condition previously to the war of the revolution:

"Since the passing of the charter, the institution hath received great emolument by grants from his most gracious majesty King George the Third, and by liberal contributions from many of the nobility and gentry in the parent country; from the society for the propagation of the gospel in foreign parts, and from several public-spirited gentlemen in America and elsewhere. By means of these and other benefactions, the governors of the college have been enabled to extend their plan of education almost as diffusely as any college in Europe; herein being taught, by proper masters and professors, who are chosen by the governors and president, Divinity, Natural Law, Physic, Logic, Ethics, Metaphysics, Mathematics, Natural Philosophy, Astronomy, Geography, History, Chronology, Rhetoric, Hebrew, Greek, Latin, Modern Languages, the Belles-Lettres, and whatever else of literature may tend to accomplish the pupils as scholars and gentlemen.

"To the college is also annexed a grammar school for the due preparation of those who propose to complete their education with the arts and sciences.

"All students but those in medicine, are obliged to lodge and diet in the college, unless they are particularly exempted by the governor or president; and the edifice is surrounded by a high fence, which also encloses a large court and garden, and a porter constantly attends at the front gate, which is closed at ten o'clock each evening in summer, and nine in winter; after which hours, the names of all that come in are delivered weekly to the president.

"The college is situated on a dry gravelly soil, about one hundred and fifty yards from the bank of the Hudson river, which it overlooks; commanding, from the eminence on which it stands, a most extensive and beautiful prospect of the opposite shore and country of New Jersey, the city and island of New York, Long Island, Staten Island, New York bay and its islands, the Narrows, forming the mouth of the harbor, etc., etc.; and being totally unencumbered by any adjacent buildings and admitting the purest circulation of air from the river, and every other quarter, has the benefit of as agreeable and healthy a situation as can possibly be conceived.

"Visitations by the governors are quarterly; at which times, premiums of books, silver medals, etc., are adjudged to the most deserving.

"This seminary hath already produced a number of gentlemen, who do great honor to their professions, the place of their education, and themselves, in divinity, law, medicine, etc., etc., in this and various other colonies, both on the American continent and West India Islands; and the college is annually increasing as well in students as reputation."

In consequence of the dispute between this and the parent country, Dr. Cooper returned to England, and the Rev. Benjamin Moore was appointed *præses pro tempore* during the absence of Dr. Cooper, who, however, did not return.

On the breaking out of the revolutionary war, the business of the college was almost entirely broken up, and it was not until after the return of peace that its affairs were again regularly attended to.

In May, 1784, the college upon its own application, was erected into a university, and its corporate title changed from King's College to that of Regents of the University. New professors were appointed, and a medical department was established.

The college continued under that government until April, 1787; when finding the attempt to establish a university unsuccessful, they were restored to their original position under the present name of Columbia College.

The original charter, with necessary alterations, was confirmed, and the college placed under twenty-nine trustees, who were to exercise their functions until their number should be reduced, by death, resignation, or removal from the state, to twenty-four; after which, all vacancies in their Board were to be filled by their own choice.

At the same time a new body was created, called by the same name, "The Regents of the University," under which all the seminaries of learning mentioned in the act creating it, were placed by the legislature. This body still exists under its original name.

In May, 1787, Dr. Wm. Samuel Johnson, son of the first president, was elected president of Columbia College. During the previous vacancy of the presidential chair, the professors had presided in turn; and certificates were given to graduates, in place of regular diplomas.

In the beginning of the year 1792, the medical school was placed upon a more respectable and efficient footing than before.

Dr. Johnson resigned the office of president in July, 1800, and was succeeded the year following by the Rev. Dr. Wharton, who resigned his office at the end of about seven months.

Bishop Moore succeeded Dr. Wharton as president. His ecclesiastical duties were such, that he was not expected to take an active part in the business of the college, except on particular occasions. The chief management of its concerns devolved upon the professors.

In 1809, the requisites for entrance into college, to take effect the following year, were very much raised, and a new course of study and system of discipline was established.

A new amended charter was obtained from the legislature in 1810; by which the power of the college to lease its real estate for twenty-one years was extended to sixty-three years.

Bishop Moore resigned his office as President in May, 1811, in order to make room for some person who might devote his whole time and attention to the college; and in June following, a new office, styled that of *provost*, was created. The *provost* was to supply the place of the president in his absence, and was to conduct the classical studies of the senior class. Shortly after this new arrangement, the Rev. Wm. Harris, and the Rev. John M. Mason, were elected president and provost.

In consequence of the establishment of the College of Physicians and Surgeons in New York, the Medical School of Columbia College was in November, 1813, discontinued.

The provost resigned his office in 1816; since which time the college has been under the sole superintendence of a president.

In 1814, a grant was made to the college by the legislature, of a tract of land on Manhattan Island, of about twenty acres, which had been occupied as a botanic garden by the late Dr. Hosack, and had been purchased of him by the state. The grant was accompanied by the condition that the college should be removed to the tract so granted within twelve years. In 1819, this condition was repealed. At that time the lands were valued at two hundred and fifty dollars an acre, or the whole at five thousand dollars. These lands, in the present map of the city, are embraced between the Fifth and Sixth avenues, and extend from Forty-seventh to Fifty-first street. The lapse of half a century and the gradual growth of the city, have, of course, greatly increased their value.

In September of 1817, steps were taken by the trustees for a thorough repair of the old edifice, which was in a very decayed state, and for the erection of additional buildings. Before the end of the year 1820, the proposed alterations and additions were completed.

At the close of the year 1827, the trustees resolved upon the establishment of a grammar school under the superintendence of the faculty of the college; which resolution was carried into effect early the following year; and, in 1829, a building was erected upon the college ground for the accommodation of scholars. The school was discontinued in 1863.

In October, of the year 1829, Dr. Harris, the President of the college, died; and, on the 9th of December following, Wm. A. Duer, LL. D., was elected in his room.

With a view of rendering the benefits of education more generally accessible to the community, the system of instruction, at the commencement of the year 1830, underwent very extensive additions and modifications, and the time of daily attendance upon the professors was materially increased. The course of study in existence at the time of making these additions, was kept entire, and was denominated the *full course*.

Another course of instruction was established, denominated the *scientific and literary course;* which latter was open to others besides matriculated students, and to such extent as they might think proper to attend.

On a revision of the statutes in the year 1836, both courses of study pursued in the college were further enlarged; and the literary and scientific course, in particular, defined and materially extended. And in order that this course, as well as the scientific branches of the full course, might be conducted in the most efficient manner, the trustees appropriated the sum of ten thousand dollars for the purchase of additional apparatus, as well as for adding to the library the requisite books of reference and illustration.

The literary and scientific course, however, as distinguished from the full course, did not appear to find favor with the public, and upon a revision of the statutes, in the year 1843, was discontinued.

Among other important changes made on this same occasion, was the adoption of the German language and literature as part of the sub-graduate course, and the establishment of the Gebhard professorship thereof, upon the endowment made by the last will and testament of Frederick Gebhard, Esquire.

In April, 1842, Wm. A. Duer, LL. D, resigned his office of president, and in the following month of August, Nathaniel F. Moore, LL. D., was elected in his place. President Moore having resigned his office in 1849, Charles King, LL. D., was chosen in his place in November of that year.

In 1854, the subjects of the removal of the college, and the expediency of establishing a system of university instruction, were considered by the trustees, and the body of professors having in view such a system was greatly enlarged.

In May, 1857, the college was removed from its old position, on Park place, to where it now stands, in East Forty-ninth street, between Madison and Fourth avenues.

On the 17th of May, 1858, a department of law was established, under the name of "The Law School of Columbia College," and a Faculty of law appointed.

In 1860, by an arrangement with the Regents of the University, and the sanction of the legislature, a union was effected with the College of Physicians and Surgeons, by which that institution was adopted as the medical department of the college.

In 1863, the necessary measures were commenced for organizing a department of science; and in the following year a Faculty of the School of Mines was appointed, which school is now in successful operation. In this institution, instruction is given in five regular courses of scientific study, viz., Mining Engineering, Civil Engineering, Metallurgy, Geology and Natural History, and Analytic and Applied Chemistry. Special students are also permitted to receive instruction in any particular branches of science which they may select.

In the year 1864, Dr. King resigned the presidency of the college, and the Reverend Frederick A. P. Barnard, S. T. D., LL. D., sometime Chancellor of the University of Mississippi, was chosen to fill his place.

In 1868, as a mark of respect to the late Professors, Moore and Anthon, two prizes in Greek, of the respective value of $300 and $150, to be competed for by members of the Junior Class, by an examination upon an entire play of Æschylus, Sophocles or Euripides, not read in the College course, were established by the Trustees.

In 1871 two Fellowships in Literature and Science, open upon certain conditions to the graduating class, each of the annual value of $500, to be held for three years, were instituted; and, at the same time, six Scholarships in Classics and Mathematics were established in the Freshman and Sophomore Classes, and the like number in the Junior Class, in Latin, in Logic and English Literature, in History and Rhetoric, in Chemistry, in Mechanics and in Physics. The next year this scheme was remodelled by dividing the scholarships in the Sophomore and Freshman Classes, by adding in the latter class a scholarship in Rhetoric, and in the Junior Class one in Greek, and by so re-arranging the whole as to make fourteen instead of twelve, each of the annual value of one hundred dollars.

In 1874 the Trustees determined to repair and improve the College buildings, and to erect new ones for the School of Mines, which work is now in progress.

Columbia College at the present time has a Faculty of Arts, a Faculty of Law, a Faculty of Medicine, and a Faculty of Mining and General Science, embracing a president and seventy-two professors and other instructors, and in all the departments more than eleven hundred students.

STATUTES

OF

COLUMBIA COLLEGE.

CHAPTER I.

OF THE PRESIDENT.

§ 1. It shall be the duty of the President to take charge and have care of the college generally, of its buildings, of the grounds adjacent thereto, and of its movable property upon the same. To see that the course of instruction and discipline prescribed by the statutes is faithfully pursued, and to prevent and rectify all deviations from the same.

To call meetings of the Faculty, and to give such directions and perform such acts as shall, in his judgment, promote the interests of the college, so that they do not contravene the charter, the statutes, the orders of the Trustees, or the decisions of the Board of the college.

To visit the class-rooms from time to time, and keep himself informed of the manner in which the classes are taught.

To report to the Trustees annually, at the stated meeting in May, and as occasion shall require, the state of the college and the measures which may be necessary for its prosperity, and particularly the manner in which the several Professors and Tutors perform their respective duties.

§ 2. He shall have power to grant leave of absence from the college for a reasonable cause, and for such length of time as he shall judge the occasion may require: provided that when such leave of absence exceeds two days, it be entered upon the minutes of the Board of the college.

§ 3. He shall preside at commencements and at all meetings of the Board, and shall sign all diplomas.

§ 4. He shall assemble the classes every day except Saturday and Sunday, at half-past nine o'clock, A. M., for the purpose of attending prayers; and at these daily prayers it shall be the duty of each of the members of the Board to be present, unless his presence shall be dispensed with by the President.

§ 5. The senior Professor present at the time shall, in the absence of the President, have the same authority as the President to command obedience, and enforce the discipline of the institution.

CHAPTER II.

OF THE BOARD OF THE COLLEGE.

§ 1. The President and the Professors engaged in the subgraduate course of instruction shall constitute the Board of the college. Professors of modern languages shall have seats at the Board only when the conduct or proficiency of students in their respective departments shall be in question, and they may be heard and vote thereon. Tutors shall have seats at the Board on all occasions when the conduct or proficiency of the students under their charge, in the departments in which they respectively give instruction, shall be in question, but on no other occasion; but they shall have no vote.

§ 2. The Professors shall take precedence according to the date of their appointments.

§ 3. It shall be the duty of the Professors and Tutors to assist the President with their counsel and co-operation.

§ 4. The Board shall have power:

To try offences committed by the students;

To determine their relative standing;

To adjudge rewards and punishments, and to make all such regulations of their own proceedings and for the better execution of the college system, as shall not contravene the charter of the college, nor the statutes, nor any order of the Trustees.

§ 5. The concurrence of the President shall be necessary to every act of the Board; and in case the Board shall be equally divided, the President shall have a casting vote in addition to his vote as a member of the Board.

§ 6. In case of the absence of the President, the senior Professor present shall preside at the meeting of the Board, and all acts of the Board thus constituted shall be valid unless the President shall, at the next subsequent stated meeting at which he shall be present, express his dissent, either personally or in writing.

§ 7. Upon any resolution, duly seconded, a vote shall be taken if desired by the mover. When the President dissents from the vote of the majority of the Board, such vote and such dissent shall be recorded in the minutes.

§ 8. The Board shall meet for the purpose of administering the general discipline of the college once in each week, except in vacation. At these meetings the Professors shall report concerning the conduct and proficiency of the members of the respective classes, noting particularly those who have been delinquent in their behavior or attendance, or deficient or negligent in their recitations, with the number of their absences.

§ 9. The Board shall keep minutes of their proceedings, and shall appoint one of their own number to perform that duty.

§ 10. In those minutes shall be noted the names of the members present and absent at each meeting. It shall be the duty of the President to cause such minutes to be laid before the Trustees at their meetings.

§ 11. The members of the Board whose salaries are paid out of the general fund of the college, shall not be engaged in any professional pursuits from which they derive emolument, and which are not connected with the college.

CHAPTER III.

OF THE COURSE OF STUDY.

§ 1. There shall be four classes of undergraduate students in college, to be called the Freshman Class, the Sophomore Class, the Junior Class, and the Senior Class. The course of study of each of these classes shall occupy a year, and the entire course four years.

§ 2. The Freshman Class shall be instructed in the Latin and Greek Languages, Roman and Grecian History and Antiquities, Rhetoric, and the more elementary branches of the Pure Mathematics.

§ 3. The Sophomore Class shall be instructed in the Latin and Greek Languages, Rhetoric, Æsthetics, the History of Modern Literature, and the remaining branches of Pure Mathematics usually taught in colleges, except Analytical Geometry, and the Differential and Integral Calculus.

§ 4. The Junior Class shall be instructed in the Latin and Greek Languages, the History of Modern Literature, Logic, Criticism, Modern History, Analytical Geometry, Physics, and Chemistry.

§ 5. The Senior Class shall be instructed in the Evidences of Natural and Revealed Religion, Modern History, Political Economy, Moral and Mental Philosophy, the History of Ancient Literature, Astronomy, Physics, Chemistry, Geology, and Mineralogy. During this year, also, students who desire it may receive instruction in the Differential and Integral Calculus.

§ 6. In each of the four years the student shall be exercised in English Composition, and during the first three years in Latin and Greek Composition also, and in Elocution.

§ 7. Instruction shall be given to students who may desire it, in the German Language and its Literature, and in such other modern Languages as the Board of Trustees may see fit to direct.

§ 8. A plan of the course, specifying more in detail the studies to be pursued in each year and in each of the departments of instruction, shall be prepared by the Board of the college, subject to the approval of the Board of Trustees; and this plan, after having been so approved, shall be published in every annual catalogue of the college.

§ 9. The Trustees shall assign to each Professor or other instructor such proportion of the time of the classes as may seem to them judicious; and the Faculty shall prepare, in conformity with this allotment, such a scheme of daily instruction as shall appear to be best adapted to promote the advancement of the students in their various studies.

§ 10. The text-books to be used by the classes may be selected by the Professors in their several departments, with the approval of the President, and with the reserved right of control by the Board of Trustees.

§ 11. The hours of instruction at the college shall be the three in each day which immediately follow the morning exercises of the chapel, and such others as the Trustees may at any time hereafter assign; and during those hours, the classes severally, or their several sections, shall attend such instructors as shall be prescribed in the scheme of daily instruction, or as the Board of the college may direct, and in the order which may be so determined.

§ 12. No Professor or other officer of the college shall excuse a class or section from assembling at the time and place appointed for lecture or recitation, or dismiss a class or section after it may have assembled before the expiration of the time allotted to the exercise, without the consent of the President; nor, without such consent, shall any class or section be excused from the performance of any exercise required of them by law; but individual students may, for satisfactory reasons, be excused from such performance, by the officers to whom they are due.

CHAPTER IV.

OF ADMISSION.

§ 1. As a general rule, no student shall be admitted to the Freshman Class, at its formation, unless he shall have attained the age of fifteen years; nor shall any one be admitted to a more advanced standing without a corresponding increase of age; but this rule may be dispensed with where, in the opinion of the Faculty, there are sufficient reasons to justify its relaxation.

§ 2. Every applicant for admission to the Freshman class shall be examined in the English, Latin, and Greek Grammars, Latin Prosody and Composition, Ancient and Modern Geography, Arithmetic, and so much of Algebra and Geometry, and such authors in Greek and Latin, as the Board of the college may prescribe. All the requisitions for admission shall be annually published in the college catalogue, and the Board of the college shall have power, from time to time, with the concurrence of the Trustees, to modify these requisitions as the exigencies of the college may seem to require.

§ 3. No candidate shall be admitted to an advanced standing until he shall have passed a satisfactory examination upon the studies which have been pursued by the class for which he applies, as well as upon those enumerated in the foregoing section; nor, in case he shall have been previously a member of another college, without a certificate from such college of his discharge in good standing.

§ 4. Every student admitted to the college will be required, immediately upon his admission, and subsequently, at the beginning of each succeeding academical year, to write in the matriculation book of the college his own name, and the name, place of abode, and post-office of his father or guardian.

§ 5. None but matriculated students shall be allowed to attend the classes without the special permission of the Board of Trustees.

§ 6. Tuition fees shall be paid on matriculation, unless the time be extended by the President and Treasurer.

§ 7. An honorable discharge shall always be granted to any student in good standing, who may desire to withdraw from the college; but no undergraduate student shall be entitled to a discharge without the assent of his parent or guardian, given in writing to the President.

§ 8. So soon as a student shall have been admitted to the college, he shall be presented with a copy of these statutes, and of any printed rules or by-laws made under them for the government of the students by the Board of the college; and another copy of the same shall be sent or delivered to his parent or guardian.

CHAPTER V.

OF ATTENDANCE.

§ 1. The attendance of the students upon all college exercises shall be obligatory, and shall be enforced by the Board of the college under suitable penalties.

§ 2. Every Professor shall cause an exact roll to be kept of each class under his instruction, and daily report shall be made to the President of such students as may be absent or late in attendance.

§ 3. Tardiness of attendance shall be estimated as equivalent to half an absence.

§ 4. A student who shall have been absent from more than one-quarter of the total number of exercises in any department, shall not be entitled to examination in that department.

§ 5. Every parent or guardian of a student shall be furnished monthly with a statement of the attendance of said student.

CHAPTER VI.

OF DISCIPLINE.

§ 1. Cases of misconduct on the part of students shall be referred in the first instance to the President.

§ 2. Any member of the Faculty may summon a student to appear before the Board of the college, and in such case he shall immediately report the facts of the case to the President.

§ 3. In case any member of a class under instruction disturb the class exercises, the Professor may require such student to leave the room; and the student shall thereupon forthwith report himself to the President.

§ 4. All sentences of the Board adjudging punishments shall be reduced to writing before they are pronounced, and the students whom they affect shall be cited to hear the same read in the presence of the Board alone.

§ 5. If it appear to the Board that the members of a class, or any number of them, have entered into a combination to avoid collegiate duties, or to violate any of the statutes, or any regulation of the Board, any one or more of those embraced in such combination may be proceeded against separately.

§ 6. No student shall be a member of any professional school during his academic course.

CHAPTER VII.

OF THE PROFICIENCY OF STUDENTS.

§ 1. Each Professor or other instructor shall make to the President a monthly report of the names of such students as may be deficient in his department; and shall also report daily those who may have been unprepared to recite, or who may have made absolute failure in attempting to recite. The President shall immediately notify each student reported as deficient, of the fact of such report.

By deficiency, is here meant such a degree of imperfection in attainment as is likely, if not removed, to prevent the recommendation of the student for his degree, at the close of the academic course.

§ 2. Each Professor, or other instructor, shall report to the President, at the end of every month, a numerical scale of the standing of all the students under his instruction, according to a standard prescribed by the Board of the College—the order of merit to be determined by examination conducted in any manner which the Professor may choose.

§ 3. Besides the monthly examinations provided for in the foregoing section, there shall be two public examinations of all the classes every year—the one to commence on the first Monday in February, and the other on the first Monday in June; which examinations shall severally extend to all the studies pursued during the session immediately preceding. Each of these examinations shall have a weight in the determination of scholarship equal to that of all the monthly examinations of the term. During the week previous to each semi-annual examination, the students may be excused from attendance at College.

§ 4. The Board of the College shall prescribe such rules as may be necessary to make the examinations a true and impartial test of the attainments of the students; and any one who shall be found to have wilfully violated these rules, or any of them, shall be liable to be dropped from the roll of the College.

§ 5. The sum total of all the valuations assigned to the performances of each student in any department, in the monthly and semi-annual reports, estimated as above, shall be taken to express the value of the student's scholarship in said department. These results shall only be used to ascertain the student's proficiency, and shall not be made public; but the President may give to the parent or guardian of any student the particulars embraced in them, so far as that student is concerned.

§ 6. Any student who shall be found deficient in the same department in more than one monthly report, may be required to study with a private tutor the subjects in which he is deficient, and to pass a rigorous examination on the same, at a time to be appointed by the Board of the College, or shall no longer be permitted to be a candidate for a degree.

§ 7. No student who, after the close of the first session of the Senior year, shall be found not to have made good all the deficiencies which may have been recorded against him in the previous years, shall be any longer a candidate for a degree in Arts, unless reasons shall appear, satisfactory to the Board of the College, to account for his failure.

§ 8. Every student, whose record of scholarship shall be found at the close of the academic course to be fair, shall be entitled to be recommended to the Board of Trustees for the degree of Bachelor of Arts. If there be any one against whom there shall appear a record of deficiency not subsequently made good, in regard to which the Board of the College are satisfied that there has been no culpable neglect of duty, such student may, in the discretion of the Board, be recommended for a degree *speciali gratiá*; and every student who may fail of such recommendation shall be entitled to a certificate stating the duration of his attendance and the degree of his attainment.

§ 9. Previously to each public examination, notice shall be given in two of the daily papers published in the city, of the time when the examination is to commence; and the Regents of the University, the Trustees of the college, the parents and guardians of students, and such other persons as the President may think proper so to distinguish, shall be invited to attend.

CHAPTER VIII.

OF EXAMINATION FOR HONORS.

§ 1. There shall be a public competitive examination for academic honors at the close of the Senior year, to be attended only by those members of the Senior class who may wish to compete. Such persons will be required to give notice to the President of their desire, before the first day of January preceding. This examination may extend to any of the subjects of the academic course; but the Board of the College shall announce the intended extent before the first day of December of the Senior year.

§ 2. The competitive examination shall be held during the week allotted to the final examination of the class; but the competitors shall be exempted from attendance on said final examination.

§ 3. The examinations shall be conducted in writing, in all subjects to which that method is applicable. Any Professor may also, at his discretion, employ oral examination as well as written.

§ 4. The Board of the College shall prescribe a uniform method of valuing the performances of the students in the examinations in all the departments; and report shall be made to the President of the results, as determined by the method so established. By the combination of these results there shall be formed a general roll of class standing in merit, according to which the honors shall be awarded.

§ 5. In the allotment of parts in the literary exercises of the Commencement, preference shall always be given to those members of the graduating class who shall have passed the competitive examination; and if the number of these shall be sufficient, no others shall be selected.

CHAPTER IX.

OF COMMENCEMENTS.

§ 1. There shall be an Annual Commencement on the last Wednesday in June, when academical degrees shall be conferred, and orations shall be delivered by members of the graduating class, who shall have been selected after the final examination by the Board of the College, with reference to their standing in the class, and their capacity to acquit themselves creditably at the commencement, viz.:

> One Greek salutatory and oration or poem;
> One Latin oration or poem:
> English orations;
> And a Valedictory.

But a poem in English, or a German oration, may be substituted for either of the English orations.

§ 2. The English orations provided for in the foregoing section shall be prepared under the following general regulation:

Members of every Senior class shall be required, as a condition of graduation, to prepare and present to the President, and in conformity with the directions which he may prescribe, on or before the first day of May in the Senior year, a written essay, dissertation, oration, or poem suitable to be pronounced before a public audience; and after the speakers shall have been selected for commencement, such speakers shall be allowed to deliver in public, on commencement day, the compositions prepared as above directed, except such as may have speeches assigned them in languages other than the English, or shall be duly appointed to deliver salutatory or valedictory addresses.

§ 3. All such orations shall be subject to criticism by the President; and the student who shall refuse or neglect to adopt the corrections and amendments pointed out to him, or who shall deliver his oration or exercise otherwise than is approved by the President, shall not receive his degree.

§ 4. Any student neglecting or refusing or perform the part assigned to him, shall not receive his degree.

§ 5. No alumnus of this college shall receive the degree of Master of Arts in less than three years after the date of his first diploma; nor then, unless he shall have made such literary progress as, in the judgment of the Board, shall entitle him thereto. The President may assign to one or more of the alumni of the college who may apply for a degree of Master of Arts, such orations or exercises as he may deem expedient; which orations or exercises shall be delivered the last in the order of the day, the valedictory oration excepted; but no oration or exercise shall be delivered unless approved by the President.

§ 6. No person of immoral character shall be admitted to the honors of this college.

§ 7. Each candidate for the degree of Bachelor or Master of Arts shall, before the same is conferred, discharge all his liabilities to the college, and also pay the fee prescribed for his diploma.

§ 8. A committee of the Trustees, to be annually appointed for that purpose, shall, together with the President, make all further requsite arrangement for the annual commencements.

CHAPTER X.

OF VACATIONS.

§ 1. There shall be a vacation of all the classes, from the last Wednesday in June until the Saturday preceding the first Monday in October, on which latter day the regular course of study shall commence.

§ 2. There shall be an intermission of the public lectures on Good-Friday, Ash-Wednesday, Easter-Monday, and on such days in each year as may be recommended by the civil authority to be observed as days of fast or thanksgiving; and two weeks, commencing with the fourth Monday in December, unless the fourth Monday shall fall later than the twenty-sixth day of the month, and in that case commencing with the third Monday.

§ 3. The President may, in extraordinary cases, grant an intermission for other days, not exceeding one day at any one time; and it shall be his duty always to report the same at the next succeeding meeting of the Trustees, together with the object and reason for granting such intermission.

CHAPTER XI.

OF THE LIBRARY.

§ 1. It shall be the duty of the Librarian to take special care and charge of the books and other property of the library in conformity with such regulations as the Board of Trustees or the library committee shall adopt; and, in general, to see that the regulations are faithfully observed. He shall report in writing to the library committee, without delay, all infractions of the rules.

§ 2. The trustees and officers of the college, the students of the Senior, Junior, and Sophomore classes, such members of the Freshman class and graduates of the college residing in the city as may be authorized for the current year in writing by the President, and such other persons as may be invested with the privilege by the library committee, shall have access to the college library, and be permitted to take books therefrom, in conformity with such regulations as may be duly established by the Board of Trustees or its library committee.

§ 3. The Librarian shall, annually, on the third Tuesday in June, lay before the President and the library committee a written statement, in duplicate, of the condition of the library, together with the names of those who on that day retain books or other property of the library, as also the names of those who are in any way in default as regards the library.

§ 4. No officer or student of the college, or other persons, shall take from the library any book or periodical, unless in conformity with the regulations, and in the presence of the librarian, or his assistant duly appointed, who shall at the time enter the title of such book, or periodical, the name of the person taking it, and the date, in a register provided for that purpose.

§ 5. No books shall be taken from the library during the interval between the third Tuesday of June and the end of the summer vacation, except such as may be taken by members of the Board of the college, in conformity with the regulations.

CHAPTER XII.

OF FREE SCHOLARSHIPS.

§ 1. The corporation of the city of New York, the corporation of the city of Brooklyn, the Trustees of the Mercantile Library Association, of the Mechanics' Institute, and of the General Society of Mechanics and Tradesmen of the city of New York, and the American Institute, shall each be entitled to have always two students; the Alumni Association of Columbia College, four students; and the corporation of Jersey City one student, educated in the college free of all charge for tuition.

§ 2. Every religious denomination in the city of New York shall be entitled to have always one student who may be designed for the ministry, educated in the college free of all charge for tuition.

§ 3. Every school from which there shall be admitted in any one year into the college four students who pay their fees, shall have the privilege of sending one scholar to be educated gratuitously in the college.

CHAPTER XIII.

OF FOUNDATIONS.

§ 1. Any person or persons who may found a scholarship by the payment of not less than one thousand dollars to the Treasurer of the college, shall be entitled to have always one student educated in the college free of all charges for tuition. This right may be transferred to others. The scholarship shall bear such name as the founder or founders may designate.

§ 2. Any person or persons who shall endow a professorship in the classics, in political, mathematical, or physical science, or in the literature of any of the ancient or modern languages, by the payment of not less than thirty thousand dollars to the Treasurer of the college, shall forever have the right of nominating a Professor for the same, subject to the approbation of the Board of Trustees, who shall hold his office by the same tenure as the other Professors of the college;—the nomination to be made by the person or persons who shall make endowment, or such person or persons as he or they may designate. The proceeds of the endowment shall be appropriated to the salary of the Professor.

STATUTE

FOR ORGANIZING

THE SCHOOL OF MINES.

CHAPTER I.

OF THE PRESIDENT.

The President of the college is the President of the Faculty of the School of Mines. He shall preside at the meetings, when present, and shall sign all diplomas for degrees duly conferred.

CHAPTER II.

OF THE FACULTY OF THE SCHOOL OF MINES.

§ 1. The Faculty of the School of Mines shall consist of the President of the college, and the Professors of Mineralogy and Metallurgy, of Mining Engineering, and of Chemistry, and such other Professors as may hereafter be assigned by the Trustees.

§ 2. The instruction shall be conducted by the above Professors, and such assistants and lecturers as have been or may hereafter be appointed under the authority of the Trustees.

§ 3. The Faculty shall have power to make such regulations for the management of the School of Mines as shall not contravene the charter of the college, nor the statutes, nor any order of the Trustees.

§ 4. The concurrence of the President shall be necessary to every act of the Faculty.

§ 5. The Faculty shall be authorized to elect a Dean from among their own number, who shall be charged with such duties as the President may delegate to him.

§ 6. In case of the absence of the President, the senior Professor present shall preside at the meetings of the Board; but no act of the Board thus constituted shall be valid, until approved by the President.

§ 7. The Board shall hold stated meetings at least once a month during term-time, and shall keep a book of minutes of its proceedings, to be submitted by the President to the Trustees at their meetings.

CHAPTER III.

OF DISCIPLINE.

§ 1. In case of misconduct in a student, unless the offence be so flagrant as in the judgment of the Professor to require the interference of the Faculty, the Professor shall admonish the offender, either privately or publicly, and, upon failure of success, may, in his discretion, bring the subject before the Faculty of the school.

§ 2. The punishment of dismission shall be inflicted only by an act of the Faculty.

§ 3. A student whom it may be necessary to bring before the Faculty shall have due notice of the time and place of their meeting, and shall be allowed to defend himself.

§ 4. If injury be done to the buildings or other property of the college, or any property used by the School of Mines, by any student, the Faculty shall have power to impose a pecuniary mulct to the extent of the damage; and, unless such mulct be paid, the offending student shall be punished in the discretion of the Faculty.

CHAPTER IV.

OF FEES FOR TUITION.

The fees of the school shall be paid into the treasury of the college.

STATUTE

FOR ORGANIZING

THE SCHOOL OF LAW.

CHAPTER I.

OF THE PRESIDENT.

The President of the college is the President of the Faculty of Law. He shall preside at its meetings, when present, and shall sign all diplomas for degrees duly conferred.

CHAPTER II.

OF THE WARDEN.

§ 1. There shall be a Warden of the Law School; and the Professor of Municipal Law shall be the Warden.

§ 2. It shall be the duty of the Warden to take charge and have a general care of the buildings used for the purposes of the Law School, and the movable property therein.

§ 3. He shall report to the Trustees as occasion shall require concerning the state of the Law School, and the measures which shall be necessary for its future prosperity, first submitting such reports to the committee on the Law School.

§ 4. It shall be his duty to see that the course of instruction and discipline of the school be faithfully executed, and to rectify all deviations from the same.

§ 5. He shall have power to grant leave of absence from the school for a reasonable cause, and for such length of time as he may judge the occasion may require.

§ 6. He shall preside, in the absence of the President of the college, at Commencements of the Law School, and at all meetings of the Faculty, and shall sign all diplomas for degrees duly conferred.

CHAPTER III.

OF THE LAW FACULTY.

§ 1. The President and Professors engaged in instruction in the Law School shall constitute the Law Faculty.

§ 2. The Faculty shall have power to make such regulations for the management of the Law School as shall not contravene the charter of the college, nor the statutes, nor any order of the Trustees.

§ 3. The concurrence of the President, when present at any meeting, and of the Warden, shall be necessary to every act of the Faculty.

§ 4. In case of the absence of the President and of the Warden, the senior Professor present shall preside at the meetings of the Board; but no act of the Board thus constituted shall be valid until approved by the Warden.

§ 5. The Board shall hold meetings from time to time, when necessary, under the call of the President or the Warden, and shall keep a book of minutes of its proceedings, to be submitted to the Trustees or the committee on the Law School, whenever called for.

CHAPTER IV.

OF DISCIPLINE.

§ 1. Complaint of misconduct in a student, must be made in the first instance to the Warden, who, unless the offence be so flagrant as in his judgment to require the interference of the Faculty, shall privately admonish the offender, and upon failure of success, may, in his discretion, bring the subject before the Faculty.

§ 2. A Professor may, for misconduct in his presence, cite the offender to appear before the Faculty.

§ 3. The punishment of dismission shall be inflicted only by an act of the Faculty, subject to approval of the committee of the Law School.

§ 4. A student, whom it may be necessary to bring before the Faculty, shall have due notice of the time and place of their meeting, and shall be allowed to defend himself.

§ 5. If injury be done to the building or other property of the Law School by any student, the Faculty shall have power to impose a pecuniary mulct to the extent of the damage, and unless such mulct be paid, the offending student shall be punished in the discretion of the Faculty.

RESOLUTIONS

PROVIDING FOR A

SCHOOL OF MEDICINE.

PASSED JUNE 4, 1860.

Resolved, That the Board of trustees of Columbia College hereby adopts the College of Physicians and Surgeons in the city of New York as the Medical School of Columbia College.

Resolved, That the diplomas of the degree of Doctor of Medicine shall be conferred by the president of the College of Physicians and Surgeons, sitting with the president of Columbia College, and shall be signed by the presidents of the respective colleges, and such others of the Faculty as may be designated, from time to time, by by-laws or resolutions of the College of Physicians and Surgeons.

Resolved, That this connection shall be continued during the pleasure of the respective Boards of trustees of the two colleges, and may be determined by a vote of either Board, and notice thereof given to the other Board of trustees.

MISCELLANEOUS RESOLUTIONS.

Resolutions Concerning the College.

ACCOUNTS OF DEPARTMENTS OF INSTRUCTION TO BE AUDITED BY THE STANDING COMMITTEE.

No payments on account of appropriations for departments of instruction shall be paid by the treasurer until the bills therefor shall have been audited by the standing committee.

TUITION FEES OF STUDENTS ENTERING DURING TERM TIME.

Resolved, That when a student shall be admitted after the commencement of the scholastic exercises of the year, he shall be required to pay such part of the tuition fee for the year as may be proportional to the time of tuition yet unexpired, provided that no deduction shall be made unless the time of admission be more than two months later than the beginning, and that, in estimating the amount to be paid, fractions of months shall be counted as entire months.

THE PRESIDENT AND TREASURER MAY REMIT FEES IN CERTAIN CASES.

Resolved, That whenever it shall appear to the satisfaction of the president and treasurer that a student, who is of good moral character and industrious habits, is unable to pay his fee for tuition, such student may be permitted to proceed without charge, or, in case he shall so elect, may give his note for the amount, payable at his convenience after graduation.

RESOLUTIONS RELATING TO A SCHOLARSHIP IN THE GENERAL THEOLOGICAL SEMINARY.

PASSED JUNE 5, 1843.

Resolved, That the Trustees of Columbia College agree to, and do hereby accept, the terms offered by the Society for promoting Religion and Learning in the State of New York, and the scholarship placed at their disposal by the said society, on the conditions hereunto annexed.

The conditions above referred to are as follows:

1. Such nominee to be of the age, and other conditions, requisite to his entrance in the General Theological Seminary, and as candidate for the ministry in the Protestant Episcopal Church.

2. That he shall have completed his college course, taken his degree of Bachelor of Arts, and been enrolled among those receiving special honors on quitting the college.

3. That he shall have carried off the prize in question, viz., the seminary scholarship, in open competition, under the judgment of the Faculty, from his classmates competing for it — all competitors to report themselves to the education committee of the society at least three months previous to the trial.

4. That such scholarship be held during good behavior, subject to the society's rules and regulations for its scholars.

5. That, in return for such right of annual nomination to a seminary scholarship entitling the nominee to the full seminary course (now of three years), without charge, and with an annual stipend of two hundred dollars, the college to grant free tuition to two annual nominees of the society, entitling them in like manner to the full college course of four years—in other words, to two free students in each class.

Resolutions Concerning the School of Mines.

TERMS OF INSTRUCTION.

Resolved, That the terms of instruction in the School of Mines shall, after the present year, begin and end on the same days on which the terms in the collegiate department begin and end, and that the term for the present year shall extend until the close of the collegiate year.

PROFESSORS IN THE COLLEGE WHO MAY BE PROFESSORS IN THE SCHOOL.

Resolved, That the professors in the Faculty of Arts who give instructions under the resolutions of this Board in the School of Mines, shall be entitled to seats in the Faculty of said school as members of the same, and shall be styled professors in the school.

TUITION, IN CERTAIN CASES, FREE OF CHARGE.

Resolved, That in the case of meritorious, industrious, and promising young men, who may be desirous to attend the course of instruction in the School of Mines without being able to pay the necessary fees for tuition, the president and treasurer be authorized to use the same discretion in admitting such students, as they are now empowered to exercise in regard to undergraduate students.

Resolved, That the president be and he hereby is authorized to appoint as honorary assistants without compensation, in those departments in the school of mines in which such assistants can be of use, any meritorious students whom he may deem to be deserving of the distinction; such appointments to be made with the consent and on the recommendation of the several professors in those departments, and to be employed as incentives to diligence as rewards of merit, and for the purpose of increasing the efficiency of the departments.

Resolved, That the graduates of the school of mines shall have the privilege of attending the lectures of the school without charge for tuition.

Resolved, That hereafter any student of the school of mines who shall have been for three years a member of the school, pursuing any one of the regular courses of instruction, and shall have fully paid up all his fees and other liabilities to the school, may, with the consent of the president, continue his attendance and enjoy the privileges of the school without any charge for tuition.

FOUNDATIONS FOR SCHOLARSHIPS.

Resolved, That every person or corporation subscribing the amount of five thousand dollars toward the fund for establishing and endowing the School of Mines of Columbia College, shall be entitled to have one student in the school without charge for tuition fees, subject, however, to the discipline and general regulations of the school; such subscription, however, to be contingent on raising a fund of two hundred and fifty thousand dollars, independent of the college.

Resolutions Concerning the School of Law.

PASSED FEBRUARY 1, 1864.

FEES, SALARIES, AND EXPENDITURES.

1. The tuition fees shall be one hundred dollars for each year for all students who shall hereafter enter the school, and for those who are now students, seventy-five dollars.

2. The professor of Municipal Law and the treasurer may, in special cases, omit the fees in whole, or in part.

3. The fees shall be collected by the professor of Municipal Law, and be, from time to time, as received, paid by him to the treasurer.

4. The rent and necessary repairs of the building occupied by the school, and an annual expenditure of two hundred and fifty dollars for the library, shall be paid by the college out of its general fund.

5. The amount received for fees shall each year be applied: *First*—To the payment of all expenses of the school except those which are to be paid, as before mentioned, out of the general fund of the college; *Second*— To the payment of the professor of Municipal Law of a salary of six thousand dollars, so far as the receipts for the year may be sufficient for that purpose. Of the balance remaining after such application, one half shall be paid to the professor of Municipal Law, and the other half shall be retained by the college.

6. The said salary of the professor of Municipal Law shall be paid in each year, three thousand dollars, on the first day of Nov-

ember, and the remainder at the end of the academic year of the school, so far as the receipts of the year shall suffice.

7. The professor of Municipal Law shall be *ex officio* a member of the Law committee of the trustees.

8. The trustees of the college shall, in all cases, on the recommendation of the Law committee, decide as to the expediency of expenditures; but they will not without the consent of the professor of Municipal Law, and to the diminution of his salary, employ any additional professors for assistant instructors, except in the department of Municipal Law.

RESOLUTIONS

CONSTITUTING

THE LIBRARY COMMITTEE,

AND

DEFINING ITS DUTIES AND POWERS.

PASSED OCTOBER 6, 1862.

Resolved, That the Library committee shall hereafter be constituted of three trustees, to be chosen by ballot. Immediately upon their election, they shall be divided by lot into three classes, so that the time of one shall expire on the first Monday in November, 1863, of another on the first Monday in November, 1864, and of the third on the first Monday in November, 1865. An election by ballot shall be annually held, to fill the vacancy thus occurring, and the member then elected shall serve for three years. Any vacancy occurring by death, resignation, or otherwise, before the expiration of the term of service of the member, shall be filled for the remainder of the term of the member whose place shall have become vacant, by an election by ballot.

The Library committee shall have the general charge and direction of all matters concerning the Library, subject always to the orders and control of the Board of trustees. They shall make such regulations as they may deem, from time to time, requisite and proper respecting the use of the Library. They shall direct the purchases of books, and shall control and direct all expenditures of moneys appropriated for the Library. They may dispose of duplicates of works contained therein, either by sale or otherwise.

The Library committee shall meet statedly at least four times a year, and also specially when called together by a written notice (of at least two days), either signed by two members of the committee, to the third, or signed by the Secretary, upon the written request of two members of the committee.

Two members of the committee shall be a quorum, competent to transact business at any meeting whereunto all the members shall have been duly summoned; subject, however, to such regulations as shall have been made by the committee.

The Librarian shall be secretary of the committee, and shall keep, in an appropriate book, the minutes of its proceedings, which shall be laid before the trustees, and read, from time to time, to the Board. He shall give to each member of the committee a written notice, of at least two days, of the time and place of every meeting of the committee.

He shall, at the end of every year, prepare and submit to the committee, a full report of the condition of the Library, of its increase, and of any losses or change in its condition during the year, together with any suggestions he may deem proper to recommend or submit, with regard to its improvement or its management; which report shall be entered at length upon the minutes of the committee, and read therewith to the Board of trustees.

The Librarian shall observe rigidly, and shall enforce the rules and regulations that shall be, from time to time, adopted by the Library committee.

No debt shall be contracted for the Library without the consent of the Library committee.

Upon the election of the committee authorized and established by the foregoing resolutions, the Library committee, heretofore existing, shall cease and be discontinued, except so far as shall be necessary to close its business, and to make report thereof to the Board of trustees.

All rules and regulations heretofore made by this Board, and now in existence, respecting the persons entitled to the use of the Library, shall be continued until otherwise ordered.

ADDITIONAL RESOLUTION ON THE LIBRARY COMMITTEE.

PASSED DECEMBER 5, 1864.

Resolved, That the president of the college be a permanent member of the Library committee.

RESOLUTIONS

RELATING TO

DIPLOMAS.

PASSED MARCH 6, 1865.

Resolved, That no diploma for a degree in course conferred for proficiency in any department of instruction be delivered until a fee of five dollars shall be paid for preparing the same; provided, however, that such fee shall not be required from any graduate of the law school or of the school of mines, who shall have entered therein prior to the passage of this resolution.

Resolved, That the warden of the law school, whenever in his opinion the special circumstances of the case may require it, be authorized to deliver to any graduate the diploma certifying to such graduation, before the commencement exercises occur, and in anticipation of them.

RESOLUTION

RELATING TO

AMREITUS PROFESSORS.

PASSED NOVEMBER 1, 1853.

Resolved, That, for the purpose of appropriately acknowledging the services of such professors of this institution as shall have devoted themselves for a sufficient length of time—not less than twenty years—to the duties of their respective departments of instruction, there be created an order of " Emeritus Professorships," without salaries or stated duties, but with the following privileges and honors:

1st. That the name and title of Emeritus Professor be inserted in the printed lists of the Faculties of the college.

2d. That the professor be regularly and officially invited to be present with the Board of the college at all public examinations, processions, and celebrations.

3d. That he have an untransferable right of nomination to one free scholarship, to be distinguished by the name of the professor.

4th. That his portrait be provided at the expense of the college, and be hung on the walls of the library, or other suitable room in one of the college edifices.

5th. That he have gratuitous access, at the appointed times, to all the privileges of the libraries and collections.

6th. That the use of the college chapel (or, in the event of the removal of the college buildings, some equivalent facility) be afforded to the professor, for the delivery of an annual lecture, on any subject within the scope of his department, in case he should desire to avail himself of such accommodations.

PRIZES.

Prizes in the College.

RESOLUTION ESTABLISHING PRIZES IN GERMAN.

PASSED DECEMBER 7, 1857.

Resolved, That, in conformity with the scheme reported in relation to instruction in the German Language, &c., two prizes for the German, one of thirty dollars, the other of twenty dollars, be awarded annually to the best student in each of the two classes into which it is proposed to divide the students; provided that, in every case, the award be made to those among the competitors in each class sustaining the best examination, the decision to rest with the professor of the department and the president.

PRIZE OF THE ALUMNI ASSOCIATION.

A prize, established by the Association of the Alumni, of *fifty dollars*, in money or its equivalent, at the option of the receiver, is annually awarded at Commencement.

Its conditions are, that it be given "to the most faithful and deserving student of the graduating class."

Three names to be selected by the Faculty and submitted to the class, who from those three are to designate one.

SEMINARY PRIZES.

Two annual prizes were founded in November, 1851, by Rev. Dr. John McVickar, and accepted by the trustees March 1, 1852, to be awarded under the following conditions:

1. The first to be entitled the Society's Greek Seminary Prize of thirty dollars, to be annually competed for among such members of the graduating class as shall have given in their names to the president at least one month previous to such competition, as candidates for the General Theological Seminary of the Protestant Episcopal Church—the examination for such prize to be held publicly in the chapel, and separate from the other college examinations.

I. The Epistles in the New Testament in Greek, "ad aperturam libri."

II. On some of the early Greek fathers, to be designated at the time of noticing the prize, or if none be designated, then upon some portion of Chrysostom or Athanasius, at the choice of the student.

The decision to be with the president and Greek professor, in the same manner as the other special college testimonials.

2. The second to be entitled the Society's English Seminary Prize of twenty dollars, to be annually competed for as before, and to consist in the production of an essay (to be publicly read or not, as the president may determine) of the ordinary length of a pulpit discourse, on some subject connected with the course of evidences, and given out by him at the time of notice, and the prize to be adjudged as before, by the president and professor of that branch, such decision to have respect to—

1*st*—The general ability and soundness of the essay;

2*d*—Its logical and demonstrative form;

3*d*—The pure Saxon style and idiom in which it is written.

Notice of the above prizes, with these conditions, to be publicly given out in the chapel, each year, at the commencement of the closing term of the Senior class, and each student giving in his name as "competitor" to designate the prizes for which he contends, and to be confined to the choice then made.

The names of the successful candidates in both prizes to be enrolled in a suitable book, to be provided and kept for that purpose, lettered appropriately, and kept on the Library table, and also to be announced with other honors on commencement day. Payment of the above prizes to be made by the treasurer of the society on certificate of the president of the name of the successfu, candidate, and the fulfilment of the prescribed conditions. The name being enclosed in a personal letter from the candidate himself, stating his intention of entering the seminary at the opening of the ensuing term; and such payment not to be taken into account, in the payment of any stipend allowed to such scholar on the part of the society itself.

The names of the successful candidates to be also recorded honorably in the society's books.

In case of lapse on the part of the college in the bestowment of one or both prizes, then the amount of such prize or prizes is not to pass into the general funds of the society, but to be specially appropriated by the Board, in such manner as they may deem best for furthering the end designed by this endowment, viz., that of enlarging the numbers and advancing the scholarship of candidates for the ministry, within the General Theological Seminary of our church, educated in Columbia College.

JUNIOR PRIZES IN GREEK.

The following order was adopted by the Trustees on the fourth day of May, 1868.

An annual prize of the value of three hundred dollars shall be awarded to the student of the Junior class who shall pass the best examination on an entire play of Æschylus, Sophocles, or Euripides, which has not been a subject of college study in that class, and a second prize of one hundred and fifty dollars shall be awarded to the student of the Junior class whose examination shall appear to be next in order of merit; both under the following conditions :

The prizes shall be open for competition to such students of the Junior class as shall have been members of the college for two years, and shall not have appeared in any term or examination record deficient in scholarship in any department of study.

The examination for the prizes shall be held within one week after the concluding college examination; and shall be conducted by the professor of Greek, the professor of Latin, and one alumnus, to be selected by the president; or by a committee of three, to be appointed by the president and the professors of Greek and Latin It shall be in writing, and shall have reference to the subject matter as well as form of the play, the title of which shall have been assigned at the beginning of the academic year, by the professor of Greek with the approval of the president. The examiners may, in their discretion, subject all or any of the competitors to a *viva voce* examination in addition to the written examination above described.

The competitors shall all be subject to the same tests. The result of the examination shall be estimated according to a scale of values previously assigned to the questions.

The student whose performances shall receive under this regulation the highest number of marks shall be entitled to the first prize, provided such number does not fall below a fixed minimum standard previously determined; and the student whose total is next in amount to the highest shall be entitled to the second prize, with the same proviso.

The names of the successful competitors shall appear in the college catalogues, and the president shall cause the same to be published in three daily papers of this city, as soon as the award is made known.

Prizes in the School of Law.

Resolved, That there be established a series of prizes in the Law School, to consist of the following sums:

A first prize of $250, for excellence of attainments in legal science, etc.;
A second prize of $200;
A third prize of $150;
A fourth prize of $100.

These prizes are to be conferred under the following rules and regulations:

1.—EXAMINATIONS.

There shall be an oral examination of candidates for the degree of Bachelor of Laws, at the close of the second year. The examination is to be conducted by the professors in the Law school, and is distinct from that hereinafter established for prizes.

2.—DEGREES.

The degree of Bachelor of Laws shall be conferred upon such students as shall pass an examination satisfactory to the professor of Municipal Law.

3.—PRIZES.

1. There shall be an examination of the candidates for prizes at the close of each collegiate year. Candidates must be connected with the Law school for two collegiate years.

2. The test of excellence shall be twofold—

a. By an examination in writing in answer to printed questions.

b. By essays prepared upon such legal topics as may be suggested.

The prizes shall be adjudicated upon the combined excellence of the essays and examinations. Diligence and regularity of attendance upon the prescribed exercises of the school shall form an element in reaching the conclusion.

3. The following directions must be observed by candidates in preparing essays :

a. The essays shall be written upon white letter paper of the best quality, with a margin of an inch wide. Only two pages of each sheet should be written upon. The chirography should be fair and legible. The essays should not exceed ten sheets in length, or three fourths of an hour in delivery, if spoken.

b. The positions taken in the essays, if debatable, should be fortified by the citation of authorities. When the point is reasonably well settled, a single decision and leading authority shall suffice ; in other cases, more are admissible.

c. Conciseness and clearness of expression, accuracy of statement, and close reasoning, should be carefully studied by the essayist.

d. The essays should be signed with a fictitious name, and be accompanied by a sealed envelope, upon the outside of which shall be written the fictitious name attached to the essay ; and within, a slip of paper containing the real name of the author. The essays should be delivered to the professor of Municipal Law, on or before May 15th.

e. The unsuccessful essays shall be returned to the authors with the envelopes unopened. The successful shall belong to the college, and shall be preserved in bound volumes for the use of the Law library.

f. Any essays which have received honorable mention from the committee of award, and have failed to receive a prize, may, with the consent of the authors, be bound with the prize essays.

4. The examinations upon the printed questions shall be made as follows:

a. Those who intend to compete for the prizes shall enter their names in a book provided for that purpose, before May 1st. If among those names there are any who have been wanting in a reasonable degree of punctuality, they shall be informed before examination that they may fail of obtaining the prize.

b. The professor of Municipal Law shall call a session of the candidates at such time, near the close of the collegiate year, as may be convenient. He shall furnish, at the opening of the session, the printed papers to the students, who shall write their answers, in his presence, upon paper similar to that provided for the essays, with a similar margin. During this session there shall be a general silence observed, except such necessary questions as may be addressed to the professor, and there shall be expressly no communication of the candidates with each other regarding answers. A failure to observe these rules will work a forfeiture of the right to receive a prize.

c. After this session is finished, the answers to the printed questions shall be signed with the fictitious name attached to the essays, and inclosed in an envelope as before. The answers shall belong to the college.

5. The essays and answers shall thereupon be transmitted to a committee on prizes, consisting of three members of the legal profession that are to be selected by the Law Committee of the college. The report of this committee will be communicated to the clerk of the college in writing.

6. The names of the successful candidates and the substance of the report shall be published in the principal daily papers in the city, at the expense of the college. Notice will also be given by letter to the successful candidates.

7. The prizes shall be awarded at the option of the recipient, in money, medals, or books; when no notice is given to the contrary, the award will be in money until otherwise ordered. The professor of Municipal Law will countersign all drafts upon the treasurer before they can become available.

Prizes in the School of Medicine.

FACULTY PRIZES.

Two prizes are annually awarded by the Faculty, at the college commencement in March, for the best two graduating theses presented during the year, viz.: a first prize of fifty dollars, and a second prize of twenty-five dollars. The theses competing for these prizes are to be handed in to the secretary of the Faculty, in the fall, by the 1st of September; and in the spring, by the 1st of February.

HARSEN PRIZES.

FOUNDED BY JACOB HARSEN, M D., AN ALUMNUS OF THE COLLEGE.

Three annual prizes will be awarded for the best three written reports of the clinical instruction in the New York Hospital, during any four months of the year immediately preceding the annual commencement in March, which shall be prepared and presented by students of the College of Physicians and Surgeons, viz.:

A first prize, of one hundred and fifty dollars;
A second prize, of seventy-five dollars; and
A third prize, of twenty-five dollars.

With each prize there is conferred a HARSEN PRIZE MEDAL, in bronze, of elegant design and workmanship, and an ornamental certificate on parchment.

The reports competing for these prizes are to be handed in, on or before the 20th day of February in each year.

STEVENS TRIENNIAL PRIZE.

Established by ALEXANDER H. STEVENS, M. D., ex-President of the College, on the following plan :

Each prize, to be awarded triennially, is to consist of the interest yielded by the principal fund during the preceding three years, and will amount to two hundred dollars.

The administration of the prize is intrusted to a commission, consisting of the President of the College of Physicians and Surgeons (ex-officio); the President of the Alumni Association (ex-officio), and the Professor of Physiology (ex-officio), in the same institution.

This prize is open for universal competition.

RULES OF ORDER.

ADOPTED BY THE FACULTY, FEB. 17, 1869.

GENERAL REGULATIONS.

It is presumed that every student will deport himself while at college, with the same propriety which he would feel bound to observe elsewhere in society. Students are assumed to be gentlemen, and they will be treated as such.

1. During the hours set apart for college exercises, it will not be in order for students to linger about the grounds, the passages, or the vacant rooms.

2. It will not be in order, at any time, to throw any kind of missiles upon the college premises, except such as are used in games of recreation permitted by the President.

3. At the ringing of the bell for morning prayers, every student will promptly repair to his seat in the chapel, and remain there until the close of the chapel services.

4. Immediately after prayers the students of the several classes or sections will proceed directly to their respective class or section rooms, where they will remain until the close of the hour allotted to the exercise.

5. At the end of each hour the bell will ring, and the classes and sections will be dismissed. Between the first and the second

hour, and again between the second and the third, there will be an interval of five minutes, when the bell will be tolled, and the students will promptly repair to the rooms where their attendance is due.

6. It is not in order to make use of tobacco in any form upon the college premises.

7. It is not in order to leave a class-room during the progress of any scholastic exercise.

CHAPEL REGULATIONS.

1. The bell for morning prayer will begin to ring at $9\frac{1}{2}$ o'clock, A. M., and will ring for two minutes, during which time the students will repair to their seats in the chapel. The chapel door will then be closed, and will not be opened again until after the reading of the lesson. The door will then be opened for the admission of such as may be tardy, and will then again be closed, and will remain closed until the end of the services. After the services, the senior class, with the officers who instruct them, will first leave the chapel; the other classes, with their instructors, will follow in order, as they may be dismissed by the President.

2. The students of the several classes will be seated in the chapel in alphabetical order, and will preserve this order throughout the year.

3. An Officer of the Roll will be appointed by the President from among the students in each class, whose duty it shall be to keep the record of attendance. Each such officer will have a seat from which he may observe the members of his class, and will make his record silently. He will deliver his report to the President before leaving the chapel.

4. It will not be in order to carry into the chapel books, papers, canes, umbrellas, or other articles unsuited to the place.

5. Should a student arrive on the college grounds after the opening of the exercises, but in time to enter after the reading of the lesson, he will attend at that time. Should he arrive after the second closing of the door, and before the close of the services, it will be in order for him to repair to the cloak-room, and to there remain until the sevices are over.

REGULATIONS OF THE LIBRARY.

1. The Library shall be open from the hour of noon until 3 o'clock P. M., every day, while the college is in session, except Saturday and Sunday, and holidays established by statute.

2. No person shall be allowed to take at one time more than one volume, if in folio or in quarto; or one set, not exceeding three volumes, if in octavo or of less size.

3. A folio or a quarto may be retained four weeks; an octavo three weeks; and a duodecimo, or a volume of less size, two weeks.

4. Any person who shall detain a book longer than the time above limited, respectively, shall forfeit and pay to the Librarian, for the use of the Library, for every day a volume is so detained, if it be a folio or a quarto, two cents; if an octavo or a volume of less size, one cent; and until such payments be made shall not be permitted to take out any other book.

5. The above restrictions as to the number of books to be taken out, and the time for which they may be kept, shall not apply to officers of the college engaged in the instruction of its students; yet they, as well as all other persons, shall be required to return whatever books they have belonging to the college, so that they may be in their places on the shelves on the third Tuesday in June of every year.

6. The Librarian shall note, in register to be kept for that purpose, the books delivered by him; the persons who receive them; the days on which they are taken and returned; together with whatever forfeitures may have been incurred.

7. Books, which, as containing fine engravings, or otherwise, are of great value, or which are subjects of frequent reference, as lexicons, cyclopedias, atlases, etc., shall, under the direction of the Library committee, be marked in the catalogue with an asterisk, and shall not be taken out of the Library.

8. No person shall, without permission of the Librarian, remove books from the shelves, nor take from the Library, any book not delivered to him for that purpose by the Librarian, who shall observe the condition of every book when given out and when returned; and the person in whose possession a book shall have sustained any injury, shall repair the same, or make satisfaction therefor, before he can take out any other book. In case any book shall not be duly returned, the person in default shall pay its value to the Librarian, or if it made part of a set, the full value of such set, the remainder of which may thereupon be taken by the person so paying for same.

9. All books taken out within the four weeks next preceding the third Tuesday in June, of every year, shall be taken under an engagement to return the same previous to that day. The Librarian shall endeavor to have on that day every book belonging to the Library in its place.

10. In the annual report on the condition of the Library, the Librarian shall render an account to the Library committee of all moneys received by him for fines and forfeitures, annual contributions, donations, on the exchange and sale of books, or otherwise, as Librarian. He shall take care that the Library be at all times well aired, and guarded against moisture, and, as far as possible, from dust. He shall see that it is carefully cleaned from time to time, as may be needed. He shall permit no loud conversation or other noise within it, that may disturb those engaged in study or research. He shall make a suitable arrangement of the books

upon the shelves; shall letter or number each volume in such a manner as to indicate its place; and shall maintain a correct and complete catalogue of all books belonging to the Library, and therein so denote them by their respective letters and numbers that any book may readily be found.

11. A list of all donations to the Library, together with the names of donors, shall be entered in a book provided for that purpose, which shall be placed on a table in the Library and remain there for inspection.

INDEX.

	PAGE
Absences to be reported	32
Admission, age of	30
" requisitions for	31
" examinations for	31
" of students from other colleges	31
Appropriations, payments from to be audited	52
Attendance	32
Board of trustees	7
Board of the college, how constituted	26
" " " powers of	27
" " " meetings of	27
" " " are to keep minutes	28
Buildings to be under president's charge	25
Chapel regulations	74
Classes of undergraduates, number and style	28
" " studies of	28
College of Physicians and Surgeons, adopted as School of Medicine	51
Combinations, unlawful, how to be treated	33
Committees of the trustees	8–9
Committee on the Library, how constituted	58
" " " powers and duties of	58
" on Prizes, in the School of Law	69
Commencement, time of	37
" exercises at	37
" committee on	38
Course of study, outline of	28
" " detailed plan to be published	29
Dean of the School of Mines	44
Deficiency, what is understood by	33
Deficient students, how to be treated	33, 35
Degree of Bachelor of Laws, examination for	67
" Doctor of Medicine, how to be conferred	51
" Master of Arts, how soon conferred	38
" " " conditions required for	38

INDEX.

	PAGE
Degrees, when conferred	37
" may be forfeited, how	37–38
" candidates for, must pay all dues	38
Determination of standing	34
Diploma-fees, resolution regulating	60
Diplomas must be paid for before delivery	38
Diplomas in School of Medicine, how to be delivered	51
Discharges granted only with consent of parent	31
Discipline in the college	32
" in the School of Mines	44
" in the School of Law	49
Dues to college to be paid before degree is conferred	38
Emeritus professors, who may become	61
" " their privileges	61
Examinations, number of	34
" for honors	36
" how to be conducted	34
" to be advertised	35
" invitations to be issued for	35
Exercises may be suspended by the president	39
Faculty of the college, how constituted	26
" " names of	10
" " their powers and duties	27
" of the School of Mines, how constituted	43
" " " names of	12
" " " powers of	44
" " " meetings of	44
" " " are to keep minutes	44
" of the School of Law	48
" " " names of	13
" " " powers of	48
" " " meetings of	49
" " " are to keep minutes	49
Faculty of the School of Medicine, names of	14
Failures at Recitation, to be reported	33
Fees of undergraduates	31-52
" of students in School of Mines	45-54
" of students in School of Law	56
" may be remitted in certain cases	52
Fines in the School of Mines	45
" in the School of Law	49
Foundations for scholarships	41
" in the School of Mines	55
" for professorships	41
General rules of order	73

INDEX.

	PAGE
Greek prizes	64
Grounds to be under president's supervision	25
Harsen prizes, in School of Medicine	71
Historical sketch of Columbia College	17
Holidays	38
Hours of instruction	30
Junior Greek prizes	65
Laws, copies of, to be delivered to students	32
" " to be sent to parents	32
Law School	47
" President of	47
" Warden of	47
" Faculty of	48
" discipline of	49
Librarian, his duties	39–59
" shall report, annually	40–59
Library, laws relating to	59
" committee on	58
" who shall have use of	39
" shall be closed during vacation	40
" rules of	77
Masters of Arts, orations by, at Commencement	38
Matriculation	31
Medal, Harsen, bronze, in School of Medicine	71
Merit roll, how constructed	36
Mining School	43
" President of	43
" Faculty of	43
" instruction in	43
" discipline of	44
" fees of	45
Missiles on the college premises forbidden	73
Morning prayer, time of	74
Officers of the roll, their duties	74
Payments for departments of instruction to be audited	52
Physicians and Surgeons, College of, adopted as School of Medicine	51
President of the college, his powers and duties	25
" shall have casting vote in the Board	27
" his concurrence necessary to acts of Faculties	27
" may suspend exercises	26–39
" with Treasurer, may remit fees	52
" is a permanent member of Library committee	60
Prize essays in School of Law, directions for preparing	68
" committee on, how appointed	69
" successful, how to be disposed of	68

INDEX.

	PAGE
Prize essays which receive honorable mention.	69
Prize of the Alumni Association.	63
Prizes, in college.	63
" for excellence in German.	63
" for excellence in New Testament and Patristic Greek.	64
" for excellence in Greek.	65
" for essay on the evidences.	64
" in the School of Law.	67
" for attainments in legal science.	67
" examinations for, how to be conducted.	69
" names of successful competitors to be published.	70
" in School of Medicine.	71
" awarded by the Faculty.	71
" founded by Jacob Harsen.	71
Professors, reports to be made by.	34
" of the college, to have no other occupation.	28
" time of, with the classes.	30
" shall not excuse classes from attendance.	30
" Emeritus, who may become such.	61
" " privileges enjoyed by.	61
Professorships, how they may be founded.	41
Punishments, sentences to be in writing.	33
Record to be kept of failures, want of preparation.	33
Regulations of the Library.	77
Reports, of President, to trustees.	25
" " to parents.	32
" of professors.	33
" of Librarian.	39–59
Roll-Officers, duties of.	74
Rolls of merit, how to be constructed.	36
Rules of order.	73
Scholarship in the General Theological Seminary.	53
Scholarships, free, how many.	40
" " may be founded, how.	41
School of Law.	47
" President of.	47
" Warden of.	47
" Faculty of.	13–48
" discipline of.	49
" fees in.	56
" prizes in.	67
School of Mines.	43
" President of.	43
" Dean of.	44
" Faculty of.	12–43

INDEX.

	PAGE
School of Mines, instruction in	43
" scholastic terms in	54
" discipline of	44
" fees of	45–54
School of Medicine	51
" " Faculty of	14
" " trustees of	16
" " degrees how conferred in	51
" " prizes in	71
Seminary prizes	64
" scholarship	53
Sketch, historical, of Columbia College	17
Statutes of the College	25
" " School of Mines	43
" " School of Law	47
Students may not leave class-room without permission	74
" may not linger about the grounds, &c	73
" matriculate before attending classes	31
" from other colleges	31
" deficient, or partially deficient, how to be treated	35
Suspensions, of exercises	38
Tardiness—two instances of counted as one absence	32
Text-Books, how to be selected	30
Tobacco—use of prohibited	74
Trustees of the college—names of	7
Trustees of the School of Medicine	16
Tuition fees, of undergraduates, when payable	31
" may be remitted in certain cases	52
" of students in School of Mines	45
" of students in the School of Law	56
Vacation, time and duration of	38
Want of preparation, to be recorded	33
Warden, of School of Law, his duties	47
" " " is to report	47
" " " his concurrence necessary to acts of Faculty	48

www.ingramcontent.com/pod-product-compliance
Lightning Source LLC
Chambersburg PA
CBHW031605110426
42742CB00037B/1237